Stitchings

A collection of stitchery designs from
Stella Whittingham of Dolls on Parade.
www.dolls-on-parade.com

All designs are hand or computer drawn by Stella Whittingham

Welcome to my world of 'drawing with threads'

This book contains a collection of over 180 designs for 'stitchery embroidery'.
No matter your favourite brand of embroidery thread, there is a rainbow of colours for you to 'draw' with.
Words of wisdom, of love and friendship stitched in colours to catch the eye and bordered with beautiful fabric create a sentiment that may be treasured for years to come.
Say 'I love you' with a lovely floral arrangement or a cute teddy bear stitchery, framed or made into a patch-work cushion. I hope you'll find some inspiration in these pages.

Happy Stitching
~ ~ Some general tips and suggestions ~ ~

Stitchings are lovely on tonal cream fabrics. Try to stay away from calico unless doing primitive work. My rag-gedy designs work well on calico.
Back your fabric with Parlan or Pellon. An alternative to those two is flannelette. It gives a wonderfully soft feel, though it does not fuse like the others.
Use a very fine brown waterproof Pigma Micron pen (0.03—.005) to trace off designs. I do not like using the blue washout pens, I find the nibs too thick and the blue doesn't always wash away completely.
Use a small 4" hoop for small designs, it's less strain on the hands.
Experiment with variegated thread colours and create something magical.
Enhance your stitcheries with some lovely novelty buttons and beads.
Use ribbons and lace to embellish or add a loop to hang your cushion.
Using coloured pencils to shade your stitcheries adds more than a little depth and warmth.
Stuff little sentimental cushions with Lavender and attach a narrow ribbon to hang in your wardrobe.
Individual designs can be made into little décor cushions, and pin cushions, wardrobe hangers and door knob hangers. Add a border or two and make a little wall hanger or tote bag.
Combine several designs with some patchwork for a larger wall hanging, or small quilt or tablecloth.
Using 2 or 3 strands of embroidery thread is customary, but try experimenting with fine work using 1 strand, or something bold, using more than 3.

~ ~

To make a décor cushion from a stitchery design, trim stitchery after pressing it. Measure horizontally and cut 2 strips of fabric to measure, by your chosen width (say 2" for example). Sew strips to top and bottom and press. Measure vertically and cut more strips the same width as before, but measuring top to bottom and sew to sides. Press. Place work onto backing fabric which measure the same, right sides together and sew all around, leaving a small opening in the centre bottom. Turn out and stuff. Close the opening with small neat stitches with regular sewing thread.
Group some small cushions with a little teddy bear, for example, in a basket for a lovely country décor look.

~ ~

General instructions for making a simple tote bag. Once you have stitched the design, sew a border (or 2 or more) around it. Press and measure. Cut some fabric for bag back to measure the same, plus 2 pieces in a lin-ing fabric—cut off 1/4" along top only of the lining (this accommodates the outer bag bottom seam and allows lining to side inside better. Cut 2 strips for the straps in your preferred length. Decide on the width you want the straps and cut your strips 1-1/2 times wider (eg for a 1" finished strap, cut your strips 2-1/2" wide). Turn in and press a 1/4" hem down one long side. Cut strips of Pellon or flannelette to your finished strap width (eg. 1") for padding. Lay the padding strip in the centre of wrong side of the strap. Turn over the raw edge towards centre of padding strip and press. Turn the hemmed side over to cover the raw edge and press. Now machine stitch down the length as close as possible to the centre fold. Sew several lines down the length for added strength.

Place the outer bag pieces right sides together and sew all around, leaving top open. Leave outer bag the wrong side out. Do the same with the lining pieces, but leave a small opening in the centre of one side for turning. Turn to right side out. Into the outer bag, place the straps, matching raw edges at top and measuring both sides equally for accurate placement, with wrong sides of straps facing out. Pin in place. Slip the lining inside and match up the raw edges and side seams. Sew all around top. Turn out through the opening; stitch opening closed, push lining back into bag, while pulling out the straps. Press around the top and top-stitch 1/4" around from the edge to finish off.

~   ~ Your creativity is fuelled by your imagination ~   ~

| Backstitch | Satin stitch | Lazy daisy stitch | Stem stitch |

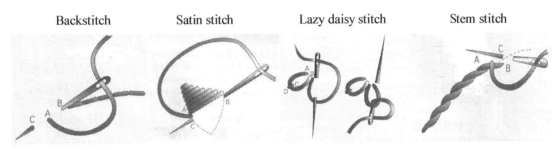

Colonial Knot

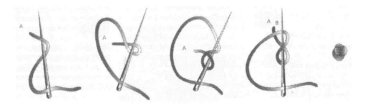

I love you

Mum

sisters
nurture
each other's
dreams

Love
is the
thread
that binds
our family
together

The path to a friends house
is never too far
to travel

My garden grows with
love and
kindness

Pins

Home is where love and memories grow

You

Forever

Friends

Me

Cherish
the simple
things

Needle
Me

Add some small flower
buttons on top of the
stems

always
my daughter
forever
my friend

Bee
Happy

Good friends
fill your life with joy
your soul with sunshine
and your heart with love
like summer rain on flowers

Prim

Primitive Bunch

An old friend
in the garden
of life
is a Bloom
to be Treasured

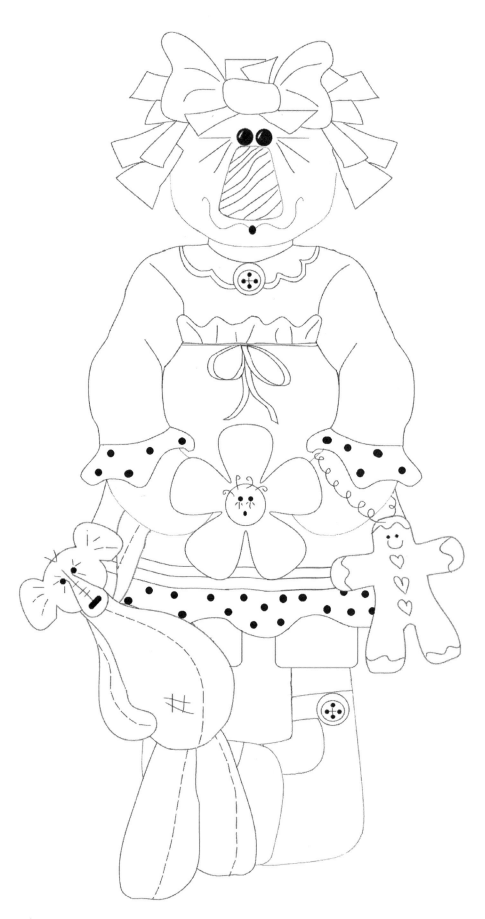

Beautiful stitched with one thread

Raggedy Friends
Forever

I love raggedy

raggedy friends

rag doll

raggedy blessings

RAGGEDY FRIENDS

FOREVER

Best Friends

Forever
my
Friend

If friends were flowers I'd pick you

Where Friends Gather

a
b c
d
e f
g h i j k l m n o p
q r s t u v w x y z

My Sister
My Friend

An Angel
quietly takes a peek
as you lay your
little head
down to sleep

It doesn't
have to be
Easter
to hug
Some Bunny

Flutter by
anytime, my friend
it's always good to see you

Creative stitches

My hands
To your Heart

Bee   happy

Thank you
for being a
great
teacher

country
home

country
hearts

country
love

FRIENDS

Flowers
are like
Friends
they
brighten
your
day

Beary warm hugs

Love iS
Beary fuzzy hugS
And warm kiSSeS

I love you
Mum

make
muSic
wherever
you
go

eedLeS

Nanna

I love you this much

Alternatively

Grandma Oma Mum

I love you

A
hug
a
day

Keeps
the
blues
away

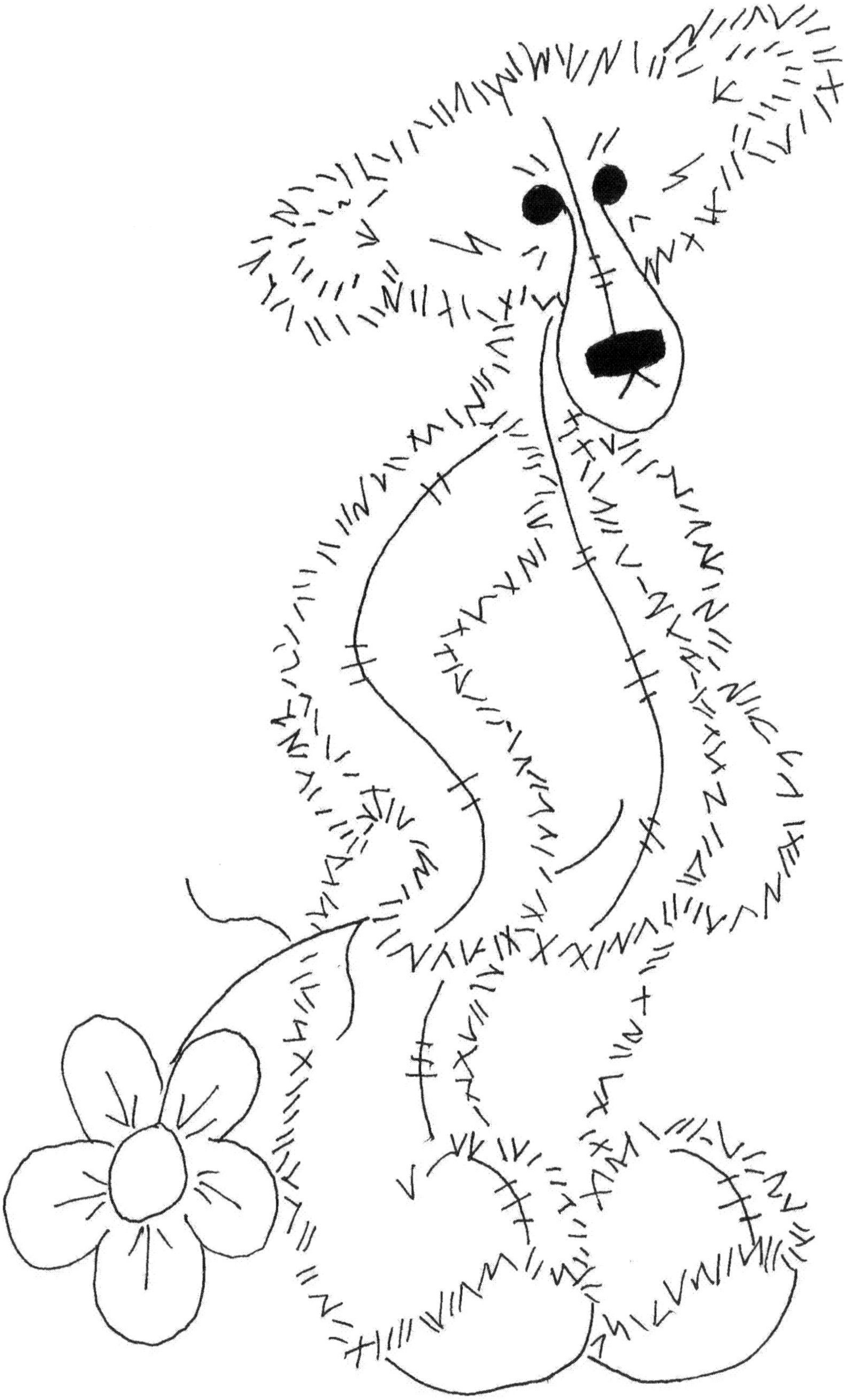

Happiness

A little Angel lives here

Add a bunch of pretty buttons for flowers on top of the wheelbarrow.

Forever
Friends

*Memories
are made
from love*

CROWIN'
ABOUT
LIFE...

A couple of country fabric borders around this chook will make a wall hanging worthy of any Country kitchen.

The greatest love
comes from a Mother's
Heart

You are so

Tweet

All that I am
or hope to be
I owe to my Mum
and her Love
for Me

Chook Chatter

My Book

Love is...

Sharing

Home

Forever
Friends

Family

A
Teddy bear collector
lives here

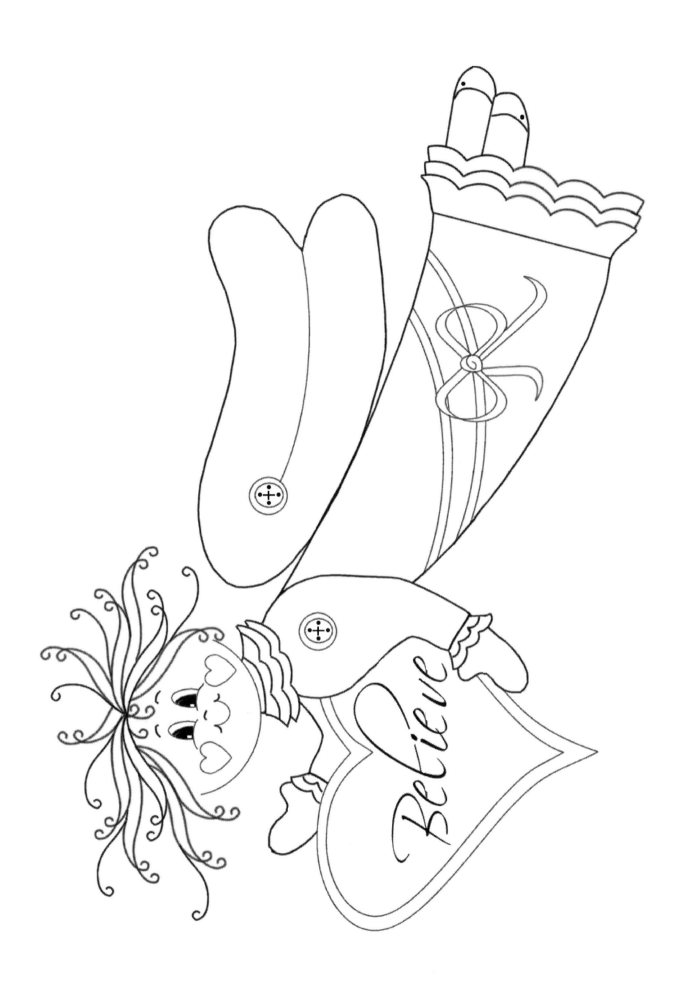

Welcome

Welcome family and friends to your home at Christmas by making this candle
stitchery into a wall hanging by adding 2 or three different borders, and perhaps
adding some novelty Christmas
buttons.

Laughter

little bear
sleep tight,
santa claus
is coming
tonight

HO
HO
HO

Merry Christmas

Have a beary
warm and
fuzzy
christmas

All hearts
come home
for
Christmas

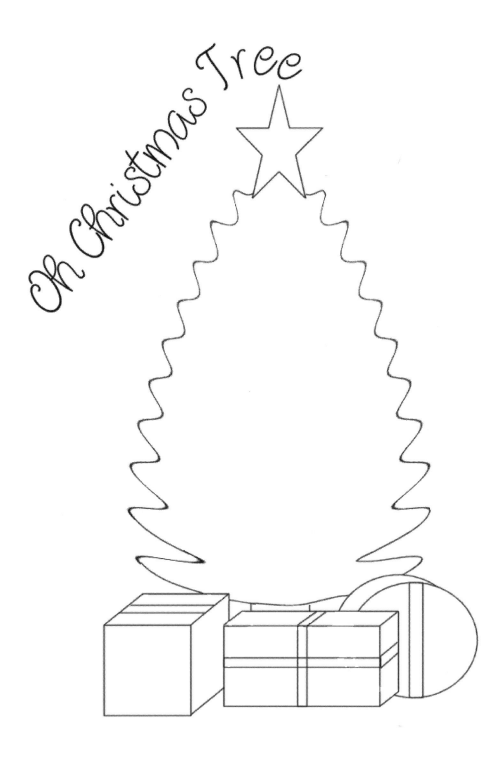

Adorn this Christmas tree with buttons and the gifts with narrow ribbon bows. Or enlarge the design and make an appliqué wall hanging.

MERRY CHRISTMAS

warm wiShes

Celebrate the season with hearts of

J O Y

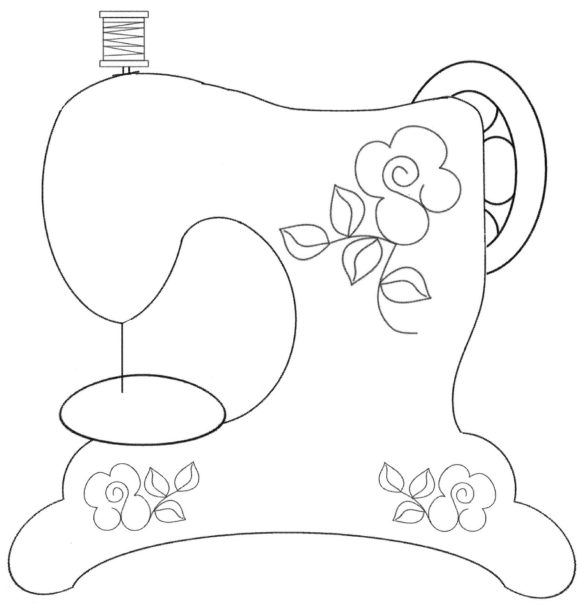

CHERISHED DREAMS
AND PRECIOUS
MOMENTS...
WITH YOU

A Daughter
is a little girl
who grows up to be
a Friend

for
you

Memories are stitched with Love

Friends
are
Hugs
for the
Heart

*All friends are flowers
in the garden of life
and mine is the
precious Rose*

Thank You

Nothing
is ever
out of reach

My mother

My Friend

love is ...

always
giving

Add pink and green buttons to represent a flower and leaves

I love you

Mum

simple pleasures

Add some pretty buttons to the top of stems for flowers

Welcome to the sty
where
on rare occasions
Pigs do Fly

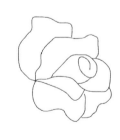
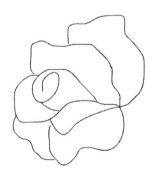

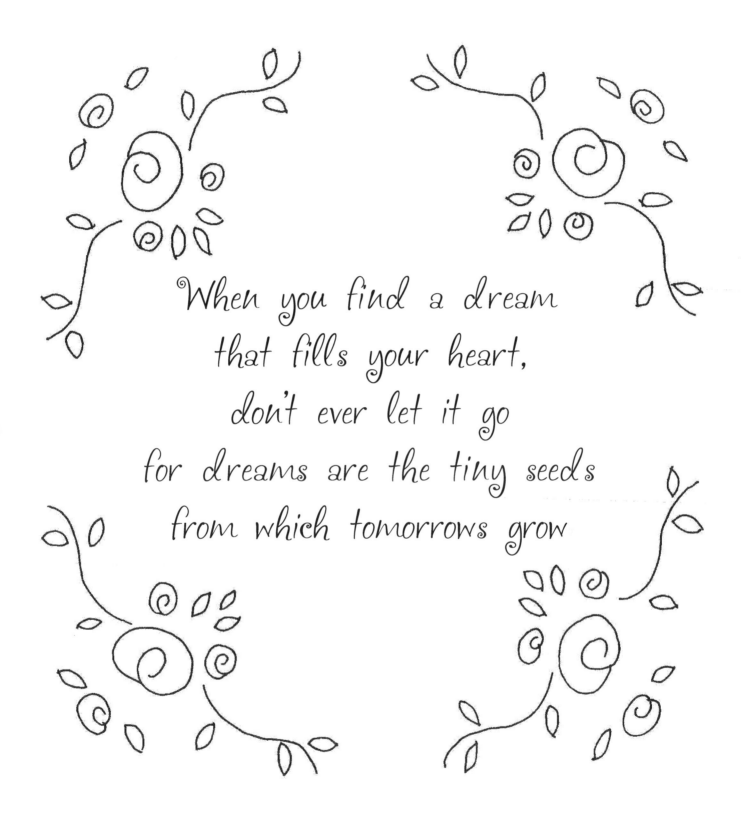

When you find a dream
that fills your heart,
don't ever let it go
for dreams are the tiny seeds
from which tomorrows grow

HAPPINESS
IS TIME SPENT
IN THE GARDEN

Best Friends
are tied together
with Heart strings

Made in the USA
Lexington, KY
18 July 2013